THE VICTORIA AND ALBERT MUSEUM

DECORATOR'S RECORD BOOK

Ɛɸ

THE VICTORIA AND ALBERT MUSEUM

DECORATOR'S

RECORD BOOK

EBURY PRESS STATIONERY

First published in 1992 by Ebury Press Stationery
An imprint of the Random Century Group
Random Century House, 20 Vauxhall Bridge Road,
London SW1V 2SA

Set in Goudy Old Style
by 𝍐 Tek-Art Ltd, Addiscombe, Croydon, Surrey

Printed in Italy

Designed by Peter Butler

ISBN 0 09175 143 8

For information about joining the V&A Club and the Friends
of the V&A, contact the Marketing Office on 071-938 8365

Hours of Opening: Monday to Saturday 10.00 – 17.50
Sunday 14.30 – 17.50

Closed Christmas Eve, Christmas Day, Boxing Day and New
Year's Day

PICTURE CREDITS

Cover background design by A. Rutherston 1881-1953, Pen
and watercolour. Courtesy of the grandchildren of the artist.

page 3 Perspective design for the furnishing of a panelled
drawing room, Anonymous Engraving, c.1930.

Cover illustration and page 7 View of the hall and staircase,
Pell Well Hall, Shropshire (architect Sir John Soane). C J
Richardson, Engraving, pencil and watercolour, 1824.

page 15 Interior of a small study, English, Watercolour, Anon.
Late 19th century.

page 23 Canon Valpy's Dining Room, The Close, Winchester
by B. O. Corfe, Watercolour, 1900-10.

page 31 Dining Room illustration from "Baillie Scott, London"
by Hermann Muthesius, Darmstadt 1901.

page 39 Interior of a Bedroom, English, Watercolour, Anon.
Late 19th century.

page 47 Bedroom by George Logar, Glasgow from "Documents
d'Architecture Moderne Vol III", Paris 1904.

page 55 French bed and wardrobe from "The Cabinet Maker"
by George Smith, Engraving, London 1808.

page 63 Design for the decoration of a side of a room, Jean
Démosthène Dugours, Pen, ink and watercolour, French, 18th
century.

page 71 Ultra-modern bathroom decorated in tropical marine
life from "Decorative Draperies and Upholstery" by Edward
Thorne, 1937.

page 79 Quaint Furniture for the Bedroom, from "The Cabinet
Maker", London, June-July, 1897-8.

page 87 Bathroom from "Intérieurs Modernes" by Georges
Rémon, French, 1900.

CONTENTS

RESIDENCE

ADDRESS
_____

_____

_____

_____

_____

HALL

ROOM MEASUREMENTS

LENGTH

WIDTH

HEIGHT

WINDOWS

DOOR(S)

SPECIAL FEATURES

ROOM PLANNER

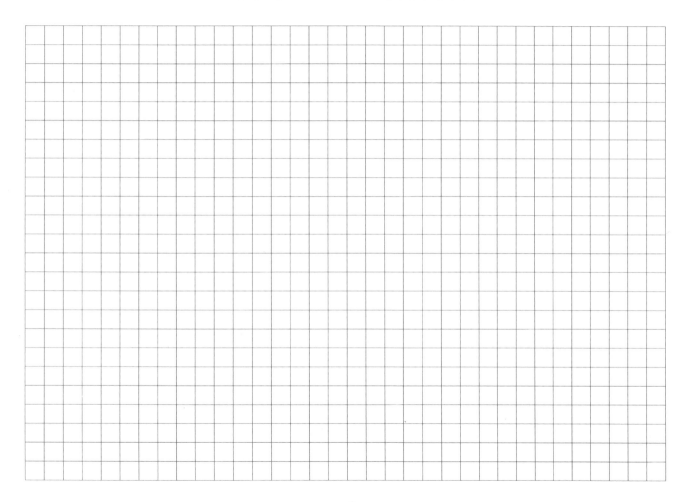

PAINTWORK
WALLS · CEILING · WOODWORK

MANUFACTURER
_____

_____

TYPE
_____

_____

SHADE
_____

_____

QUANTITY
_____

_____

PRICE
_____

_____

SUPPLIER
_____

_____

_____

WALLPAPER
WALLS · CEILING · STAIRWAY

MANUFACTURER

TYPE

SHADE / PATTERN

QUANTITY

PRICE

SUPPLIER

FLOOR COVERINGS
CARPETS · TILES · OTHER

MANUFACTURER
_____

TYPE
_____

_____

SHADE / PATTERN
_____

_____

QUANTITY
_____

_____

PRICE
_____

_____

SUPPLIER
_____

_____

SPECIAL FEATURES
_____

_____

FURNITURE PLANNER

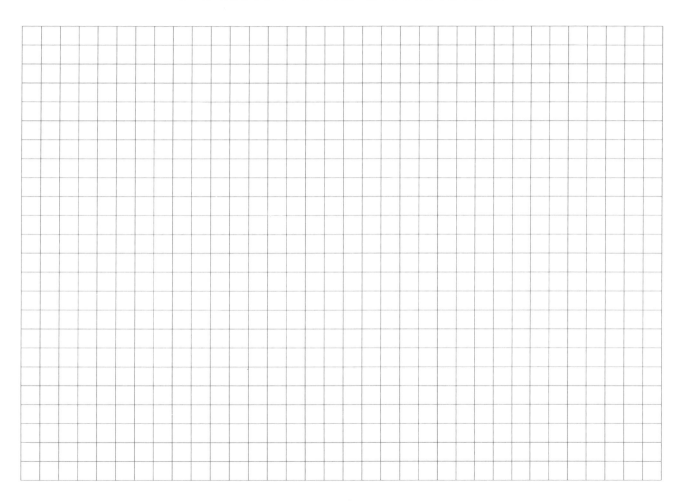

FABRICS
WINDOWS · CHAIRS

MANUFACTURER
_____

_____

TYPE
_____

_____

SHADE / PATTERN
_____

_____

QUANTITY
_____

_____

PRICE
_____

_____

SUPPLIER
_____

_____

ROOM COMPLETION DATE
_____

LIVING ROOM

ROOM MEASUREMENTS

LENGTH

WIDTH

HEIGHT

WINDOWS

DOOR(S)

SPECIAL FEATURES

ROOM PLANNER

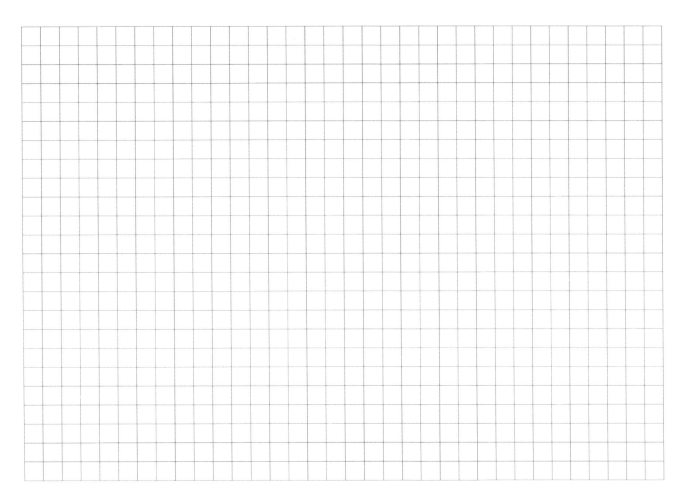

PAINTWORK
WALLS · CEILING · WOODWORK

MANUFACTURER

_____

_____

TYPE

_____

_____

SHADE

_____

_____

QUANTITY

_____

_____

PRICE

_____

_____

SUPPLIER

_____

_____

WALLPAPER
WALLS · CEILING

MANUFACTURER
_____

_____

TYPE
_____

_____

SHADE / PATTERN
_____

_____

QUANTITY
_____

_____

PRICE
_____

_____

SUPPLIER
_____

_____

FLOOR COVERINGS
CARPETS · TILES · OTHER

MANUFACTURER

TYPE

SHADE / PATTERN

QUANTITY

PRICE

SUPPLIER

SPECIAL FEATURES

FURNITURE PLANNER

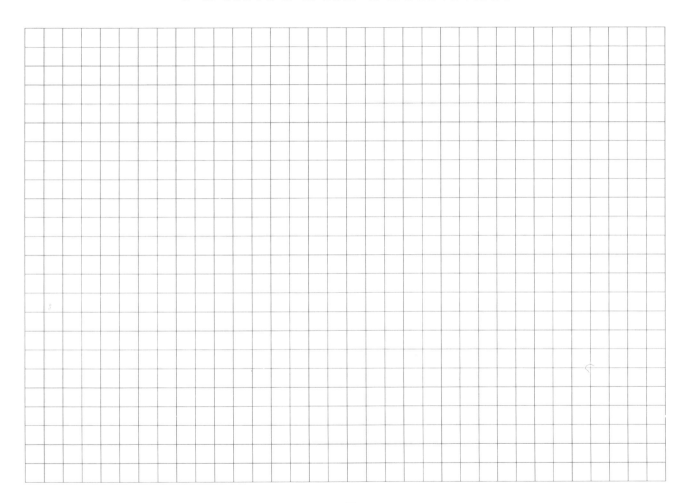

FABRICS
WALLS · UPHOLSTERY · CUSHIONS

MANUFACTURER

TYPE

SHADE / PATTERN

QUANTITY

PRICE

SUPPLIER

ROOM COMPLETION DATE

DINING ROOM

ROOM MEASUREMENTS

LENGTH
_____

_____

WIDTH
_____

_____

HEIGHT
_____

_____

WINDOWS
_____

_____

DOOR(S)
_____

_____

SPECIAL FEATURES
_____

_____

_____

ROOM PLANNER

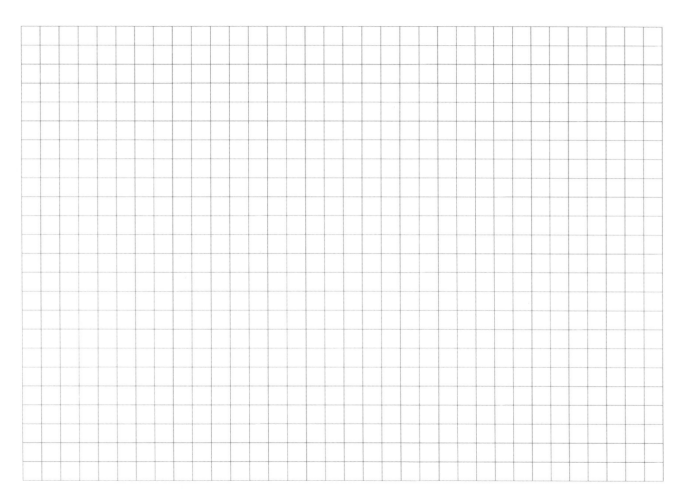

PAINTWORK
WALLS · CEILING · WOODWORK

MANUFACTURER

TYPE

SHADE

QUANTITY

PRICE

SUPPLIER

WALLPAPER
WALLS · CEILING

MANUFACTURER

TYPE

SHADE / PATTERN

QUANTITY

PRICE

SUPPLIER

FLOOR COVERINGS
CARPETS · TILES · OTHER

MANUFACTURER

TYPE

SHADE / PATTERN

QUANTITY

PRICE

SUPPLIER

SPECIAL FEATURES

FURNITURE PLANNER

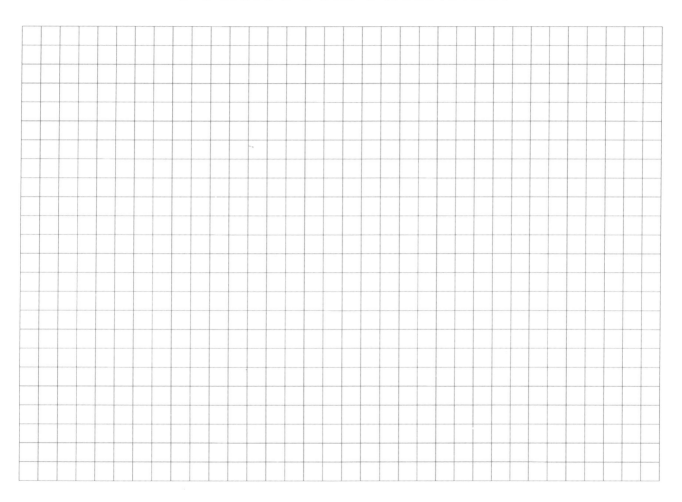

FABRICS
WALLS · UPHOLSTERY · CUSHIONS

MANUFACTURER
_____

_____

TYPE
_____

_____

SHADE / PATTERN
_____

_____

QUANTITY
_____

_____

PRICE
_____

_____

SUPPLIER
_____

_____

ROOM COMPLETION DATE
_____

KITCHEN

ROOM MEASUREMENTS

LENGTH

WIDTH

HEIGHT

WINDOWS

DOOR(S)

SPECIAL FEATURES

ROOM PLANNER

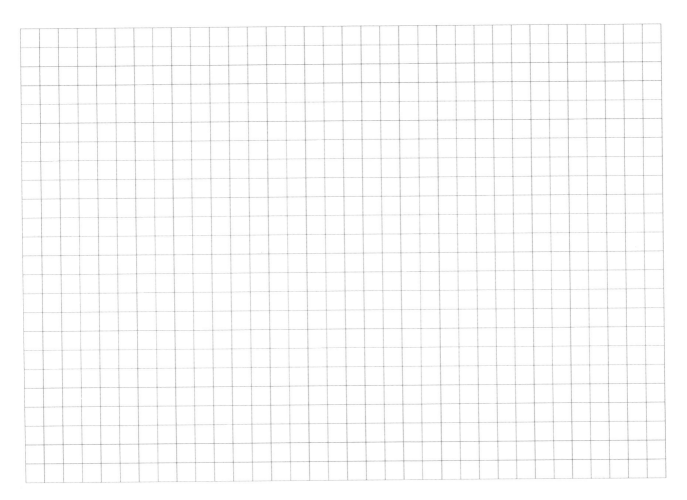

PAINTWORK
WALLS · CEILING · WOODWORK

MANUFACTURER

TYPE

SHADE

QUANTITY

PRICE

SUPPLIER

WALLPAPER
WALLS · CEILING

MANUFACTURER

TYPE

SHADE / PATTERN

QUANTITY

PRICE

SUPPLIER

FLOOR COVERINGS
CARPETS · TILES · OTHER

MANUFACTURER

TYPE

SHADE / PATTERN

QUANTITY

PRICE

SUPPLIER

SPECIAL FEATURES

FURNITURE PLANNER

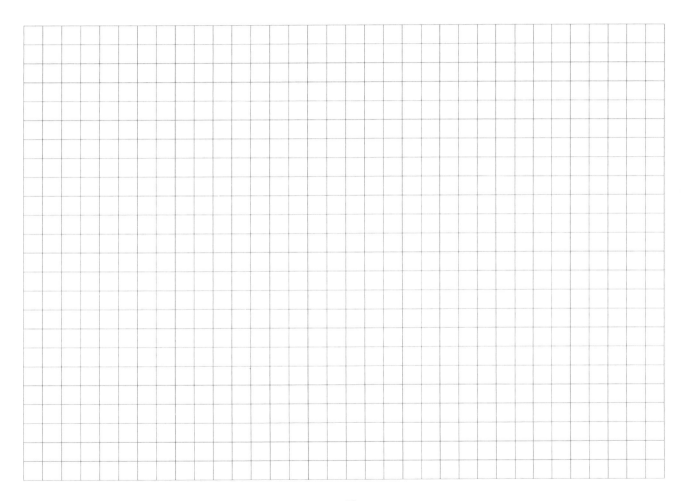

FABRIC AND OTHER COVERINGS
WINDOWS · UPHOLSTERY · WORK SURFACES

MANUFACTURER

CLOTH / OTHER

SHADE / PATTERN

QUANTITY

PRICE

SUPPLIER

ROOM COMPLETION DATE

BEDROOM 1

ROOM MEASUREMENTS

LENGTH
_____

_____

WIDTH
_____

_____

HEIGHT
_____

_____

WINDOWS
_____

_____

DOOR(S)
_____

_____

SPECIAL FEATURES
_____

_____

ROOM PLANNER

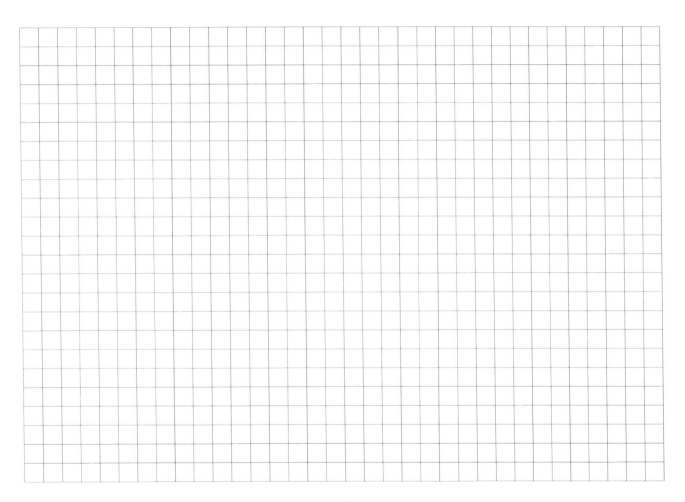

PAINTWORK
WALLS · CEILING · WOODWORK

MANUFACTURER

TYPE

SHADE

QUANTITY

PRICE

SUPPLIER

WALLPAPER
WALLS · CEILING

MANUFACTURER

TYPE

SHADE / PATTERN

QUANTITY

PRICE

SUPPLIER

FLOOR COVERINGS
CARPETS · OTHER

MANUFACTURER

TYPE

SHADE / PATTERN

QUANTITY

PRICE

SUPPLIER

SPECIAL FEATURES

FURNITURE PLANNER

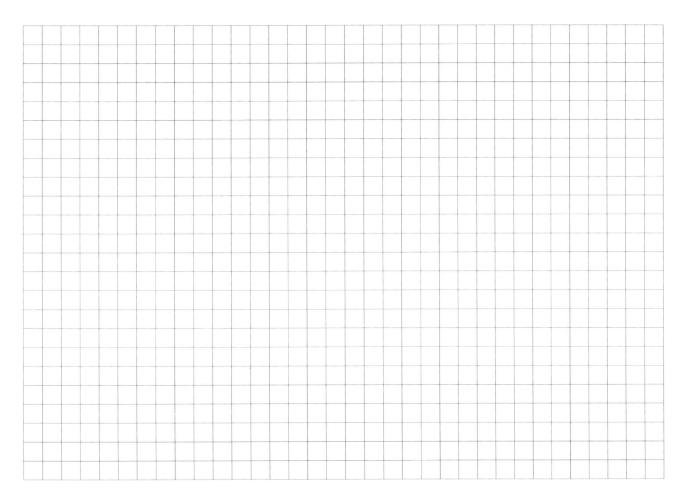

FABRICS
WINDOWS · CHAIRS · BEDCOVERINGS

MANUFACTURER

TYPE

SHADE / PATTERN

QUANTITY

PRICE

SUPPLIER

ROOM COMPLETION DATE

BEDROOM 2

ROOM MEASUREMENTS

LENGTH
_____

_____

WIDTH
_____

_____

HEIGHT
_____

_____

WINDOWS
_____

_____

DOOR(S)
_____

_____

SPECIAL FEATURES
_____

_____

_____

ROOM PLANNER

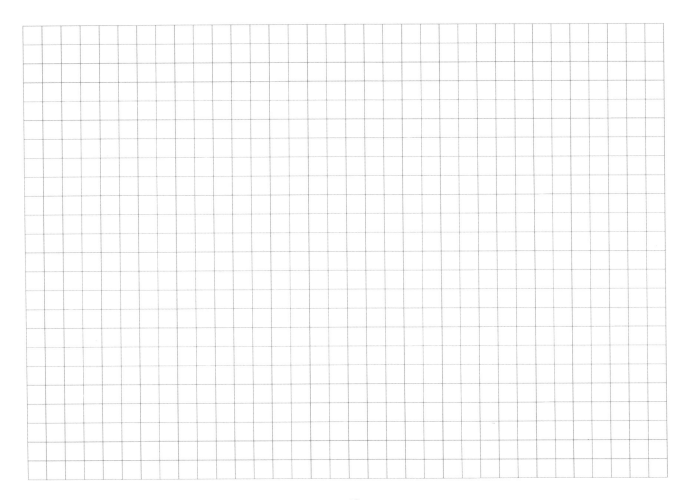

PAINTWORK
WALLS · CEILING · WOODWORK

MANUFACTURER

TYPE

SHADE

QUANTITY

PRICE

SUPPLIER

WALLPAPER
WALLS · CEILING

MANUFACTURER

TYPE

SHADE / PATTERN

QUANTITY

PRICE

SUPPLIER

FLOOR COVERINGS
CARPETS · OTHER

MANUFACTURER

TYPE

SHADE / PATTERN

QUANTITY

PRICE

SUPPLIER

SPECIAL FEATURES

FURNITURE PLANNER

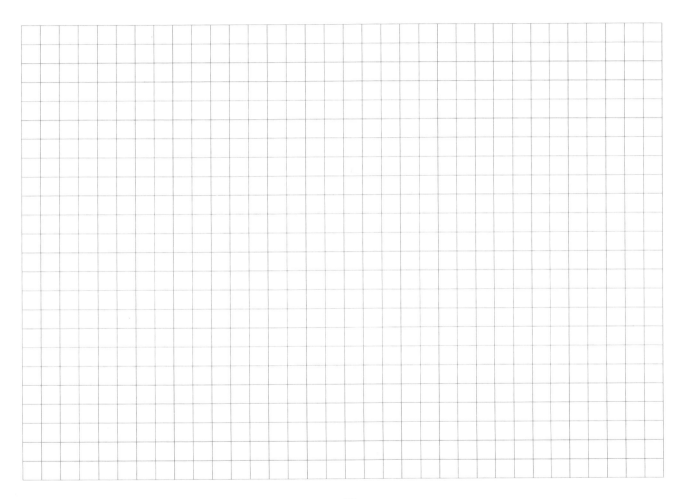

FABRICS

WINDOWS · CHAIRS · BEDCOVERINGS

MANUFACTURER

TYPE

SHADE / PATTERN

QUANTITY

PRICE

SUPPLIER

ROOM COMPLETION DATE

BEDROOM 3

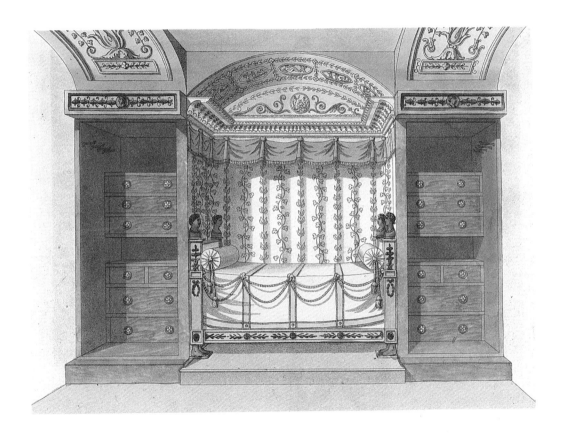

ROOM MEASUREMENTS

LENGTH
_____

_____

WIDTH
_____

_____

HEIGHT
_____

_____

WINDOWS
_____

_____

DOOR(S)
_____

_____

SPECIAL FEATURES
_____

_____

_____

ROOM PLANNER

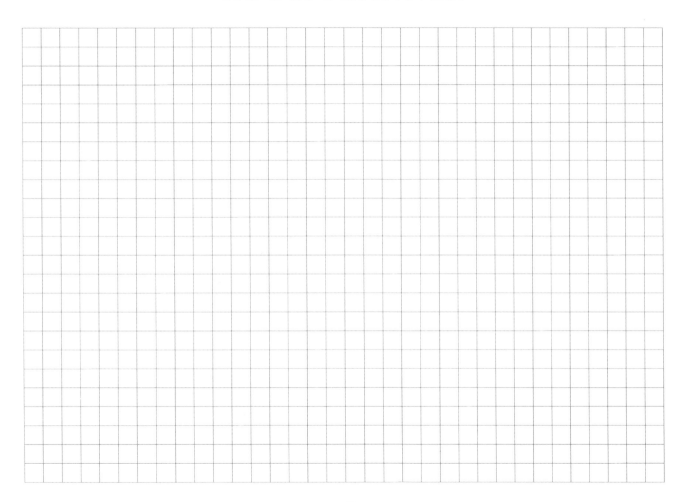

PAINTWORK
WALLS · CEILING · WOODWORK

MANUFACTURER

_____

TYPE

_____

SHADE

_____

QUANTITY

_____

PRICE

_____

SUPPLIER

_____

WALLPAPER
WALLS · CEILING

MANUFACTURER
_____

_____

TYPE
_____

_____

SHADE / PATTERN
_____

_____

QUANTITY
_____

_____

PRICE
_____

_____

SUPPLIER
_____

_____

FLOOR COVERINGS
CARPETS · OTHER

MANUFACTURER
_____

TYPE
_____

_____

SHADE / PATTERN
_____

_____

QUANTITY
_____

_____

PRICE
_____

_____

SUPPLIER
_____

_____

SPECIAL FEATURES
_____

_____

FURNITURE PLANNER

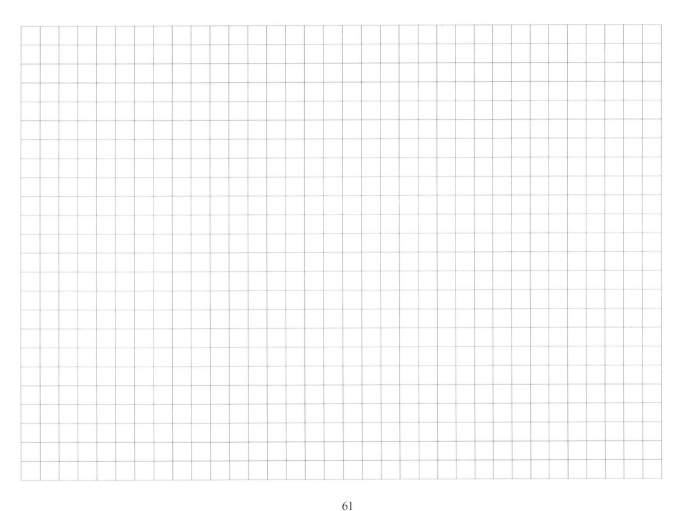

FABRICS
WINDOWS · CHAIRS · BEDCOVERINGS

MANUFACTURER

TYPE

SHADE / PATTERN

QUANTITY

PRICE

SUPPLIER

ROOM COMPLETION DATE

BEDROOM 4

ROOM MEASUREMENTS

LENGTH

WIDTH

HEIGHT

WINDOWS

DOOR(S)

SPECIAL FEATURES

ROOM PLANNER

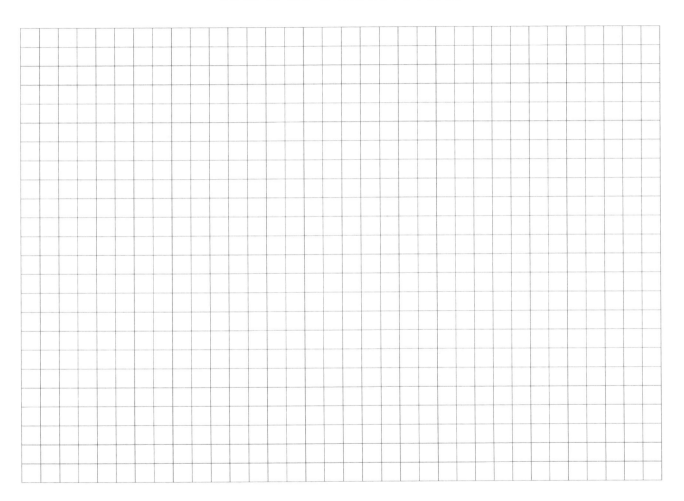

PAINTWORK
WALLS · CEILING · WOODWORK

MANUFACTURER

TYPE

SHADE

QUANTITY

PRICE

SUPPLIER

WALLPAPER
WALLS · CEILING

MANUFACTURER

TYPE

SHADE / PATTERN

QUANTITY

PRICE

SUPPLIER

FLOOR COVERINGS
CARPETS · OTHER

MANUFACTURER

TYPE

SHADE / PATTERN

QUANTITY

PRICE

SUPPLIER

SPECIAL FEATURES

FURNITURE PLANNER

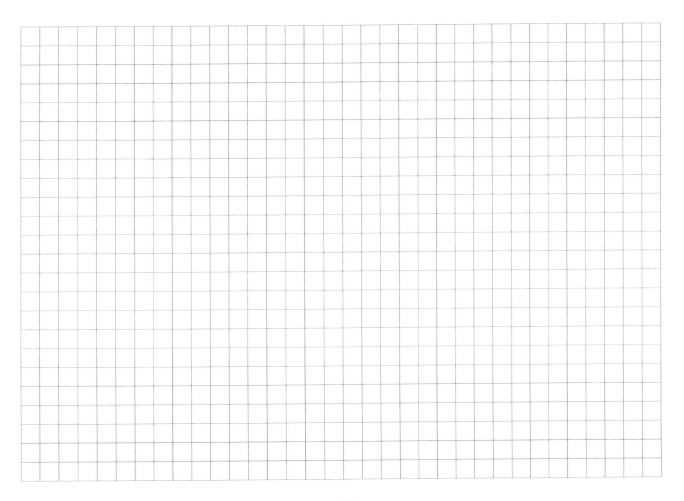

FABRICS
WINDOWS · CHAIRS · BEDCOVERINGS

MANUFACTURER

TYPE

SHADE / PATTERN

QUANTITY

PRICE

SUPPLIER

ROOM COMPLETION DATE

BATHROOM 1

ROOM MEASUREMENTS

LENGTH
_____

_____

WIDTH
_____

_____

HEIGHT
_____

_____

WINDOWS
_____

_____

DOOR(S)
_____

_____

SPECIAL FEATURES
_____

_____

_____

ROOM PLANNER

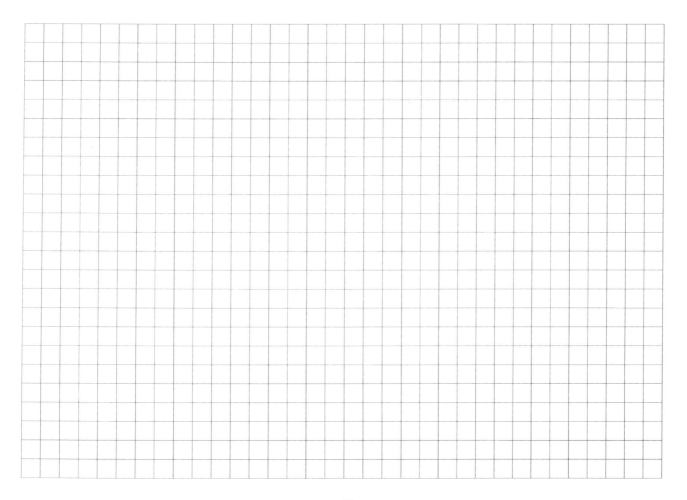

PAINTWORK
WALLS · CEILING · WOODWORK

MANUFACTURER

TYPE

SHADE

QUANTITY

PRICE

SUPPLIER

WALLPAPER
WALLS · CEILING

MANUFACTURER

TYPE

SHADE / PATTERN

QUANTITY

PRICE

SUPPLIER

FLOOR COVERINGS

TILES · OTHER

MANUFACTURER

_____

TYPE

_____

SHADE / PATTERN

_____

QUANTITY

_____

PRICE

_____

SUPPLIER

_____

FURNITURE PLANNER

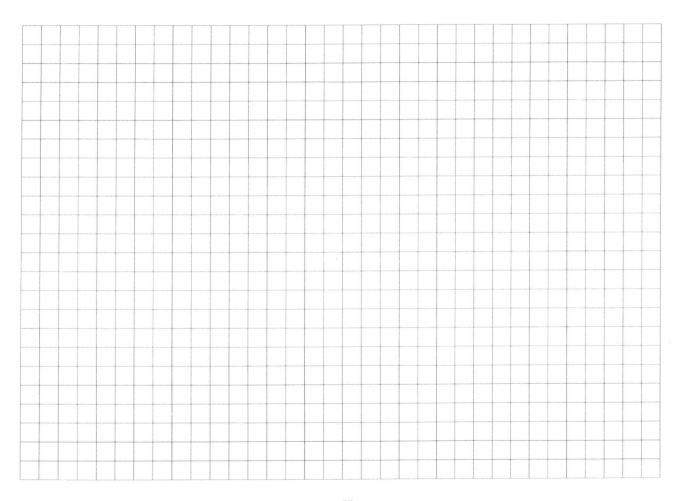

ACCESSORIES
WINDOWS · TOWELS · OTHER

MANUFACTURER

TYPE

SHADE / PATTERN

QUANTITY

PRICE

SUPPLIER

ROOM COMPLETION DATE

BATHROOM 2

ROOM MEASUREMENTS

LENGTH
_____

_____

WIDTH
_____

_____

HEIGHT
_____

_____

WINDOWS
_____

_____

DOOR(S)
_____

_____

SPECIAL FEATURES
_____

_____

_____

ROOM PLANNER

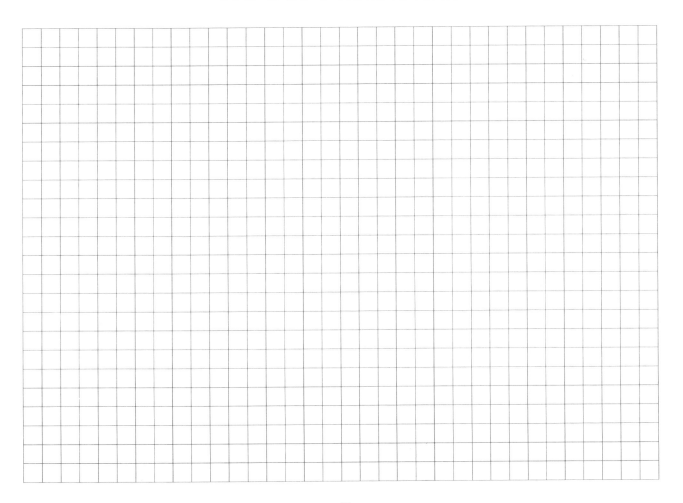

PAINTWORK
WALLS · CEILING · WOODWORK

MANUFACTURER

TYPE

SHADE

QUANTITY

PRICE

SUPPLIER

WALLPAPER
WALLS · CEILING

MANUFACTURER

TYPE

SHADE / PATTERN

QUANTITY

PRICE

SUPPLIER

FLOOR COVERINGS
TILES · OTHER

MANUFACTURER

TYPE

SHADE / PATTERN

QUANTITY

PRICE

SUPPLIER

FURNITURE PLANNER

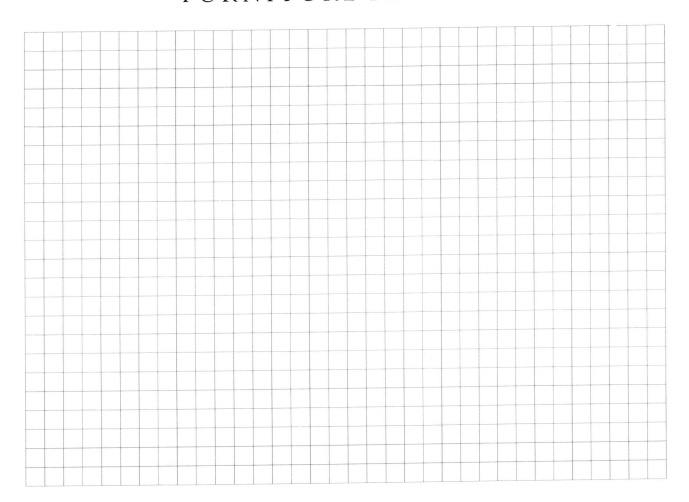

ACCESSORIES
WINDOWS · TOWELS · OTHER

MANUFACTURER

TYPE

SHADE / PATTERN

QUANTITY

PRICE

SUPPLIER

ROOM COMPLETION DATE

AN EXTRA ROOM

ROOM MEASUREMENTS

LENGTH

_____

_____

WIDTH

_____

_____

HEIGHT

_____

_____

WINDOWS

_____

_____

DOOR(S)

_____

_____

SPECIAL FEATURES

_____

_____

ROOM PLANNER

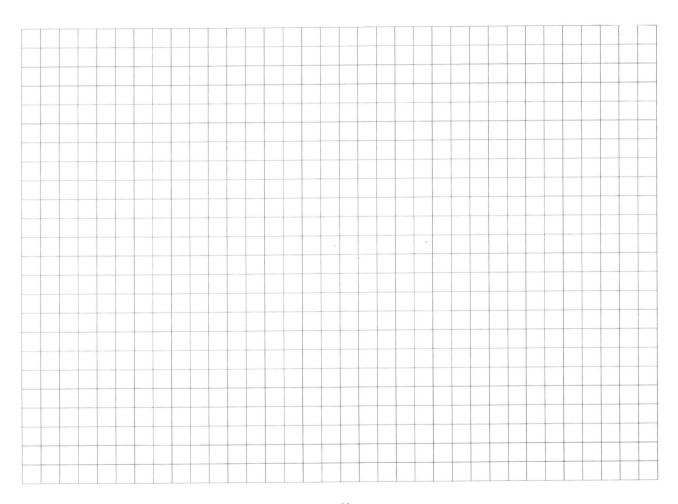

PAINTWORK
WALLS · CEILING · WOODWORK

MANUFACTURER

TYPE

SHADE

QUANTITY

PRICE

SUPPLIER

WALLPAPER
WALLS · CEILING

MANUFACTURER

TYPE

SHADE / PATTERN

QUANTITY

PRICE

SUPPLIER

FLOOR COVERINGS
CARPETS · TILES · OTHER

MANUFACTURER

TYPE

SHADE / PATTERN

QUANTITY

PRICE

SUPPLIER

SPECIAL FEATURES

FURNITURE PLANNER

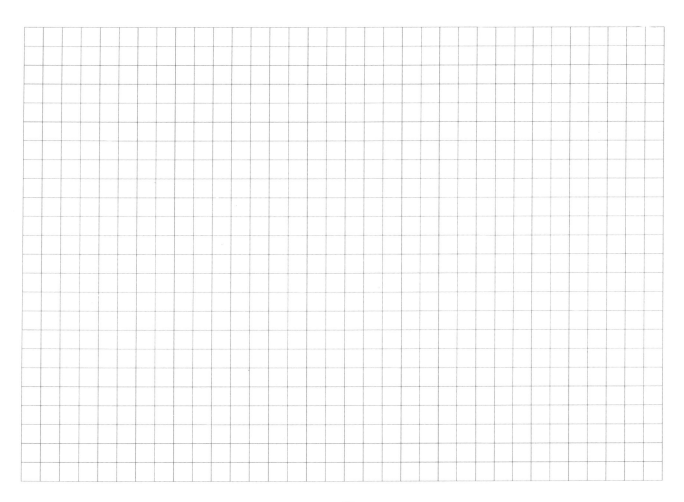

FABRICS
WALLS · UPHOLSTERY · CUSHIONS

MANUFACTURER
_____

_____

TYPE
_____

_____

SHADE / PATTERN
_____

_____

QUANTITY
_____

_____

PRICE
_____

_____

SUPPLIER
_____

_____

ROOM COMPLETION DATE
_____

ADDRESSES

TYPE OF SUPPLIER

NAME

ADDRESS

TELEPHONE

TYPE OF SUPPLIER

NAME

ADDRESS

TELEPHONE

TYPE OF SUPPLIER

NAME

ADDRESS

TELEPHONE

TYPE OF SUPPLIER

NAME

ADDRESS

TELEPHONE

TYPE OF SUPPLIER

NAME

ADDRESS

TELEPHONE

TYPE OF SUPPLIER

NAME

ADDRESS

TELEPHONE

TYPE OF SUPPLIER

NAME

ADDRESS

TELEPHONE

TYPE OF SUPPLIER

NAME

ADDRESS

TELEPHONE